Digging Up Dinosaur Fossils in

Australia

Little Mitchie
an imprint of Mitchell Lane

Digging Up Dinosaur Fossils

Creating Young Nonfiction Readers

Little Mitchie lets children delve into nonfiction at beginning reading levels. Young readers are introduced to new concepts, facts, ideas, and vocabulary.

Tips for Reading Nonfiction with Young Readers

Talk about Nonfiction

Begin by explaining that nonfiction books give us information that is true. The book will be organized around a specific topic or idea, and we may learn new facts through reading.

Look at the Parts

Most nonfiction books have helpful features. Our *Little Mitchie* titles include color photographs and graphic aids, a table of contents, a glossary, and an index. Share the purpose of these features with your reader.

Color Photos and Graphic Aids

A lot of information can be found by "reading" photos, charts, maps, and other graphic aids found within nonfiction texts. Help your reader learn more about the different ways information can be displayed.

Table of Contents

Located at the front of the book, this list shows the big ideas within the text and the page numbers where they can be found.

Glossary

Located at the back of the book, the glossary defines key words and phrases that are related to the topic. These words and phrases can be found in the text in colored type.

Index

Located at the back of the book, an index is an alphabetical list of topics and the page numbers where they can be found.

With a little help and guidance about reading nonfiction, you can feel good about introducing a young reader to the world of *Little Mitchie* nonfiction books.

Mitchell Lane
PUBLISHERS

2001 SW 31st Avenue
Hallandale, FL 33009
www.mitchelllanepub.com

Little Mitchie

First Edition, 2025.

Author: Meg Greve
Designer: Rhea Magaro
Editor: Madison Greve

Names/credits:
Title: Digging Up Dinosaur Fossils in Australia / by Meg Greve
Description: Hallandale, FL : Mitchell Lane Publishers, [2025]

Series: Digging Up Dinosaur Fossils
Library bound ISBN: 979-8-89260-240-2
Paperback ISBN: 979-8-89260-417-8
eBook ISBN: 979-8-89260-247-1

Little Mitchie is an imprint of Mitchell Lane Publishers.

PHOTO CREDITS
Alamy: Stocktrek Images, Inc., 8-9, 14-15; NDK, 14; Universal Images Group North America LLC/DeAgostini, 16-17; Shutterstock: Michael Rosskothen, cover, 1, 3, 10-11, 18-19; Colorcocktail, cover, 1 (sign); Aust28, 4, 6, 9, 11, 13, 15, 17, 18, 20, 23; Noiel, 5; Engineer studio, 6-7; Kat Om, 20-21; Wiki: 12-13

CONTENTS

When Dinosaurs Ruled the Land

The air is wet and cool. Trees with sharp needles and Earth's first flowers fill the forests. But where are the kangaroos and koalas? Not here! This was Australia before it was a **continent**. This was the time of the dinosaurs!

Before there were seven continents, all land formed one giant continent called Pangea.

Before there were humans, dinosaurs ruled the earth. Paleontologists are scientists who study the **fossils** of these mighty animals. They teach us about the earth and how dinosaurs lived, over 200 million years ago.

DINO DETAILS:
Australovenator belonged to a group of dinosaurs that all had large, sharp claws. They used their claws like fingers, to grab food such as turtles and crocodiles.

Meat for Dinner? Meet the Carnivores!

Australovenator was a fearsome **carnivore**. It had huge claws that were as big as its hands. Since its fossils were found in Australia, it was given the nickname "southern hunter."

DINO DETAILS:
During the time of the dinosaurs, all of Earth's land was connected. But dinosaurs of the same kind liked to stick to the lands that they knew the best.

Cryolophosaurus walked on its hind legs and had a crest on top of its head. It lived on land that is now Antarctica. During this time, Australia was connected to this land.

DINO DETAILS:

Even dinosaurs with three toes on each foot could have probably outrun and outhunted any human.

Imperobator lived in the land connecting Antarctica and Australia. It was one of only two kinds of dinosaurs in this region to walk on hind legs. It had three toes on each foot. Many believe that it was more than 6 feet (2 meters) tall.

DINO DETAILS:

Based on teeth shape, scientists are able to guess whether certain dinosaurs ate plants, meat, or both! because of the shape of Muttaburrasaurus's teeth, there is a chance it may have eaten both meat and plants.

More Plants for the Herbivores, Please!

Muttaburrasaurus was a plant-eating **herbivore** with a very strange name. It also had a very strange head! Its snout was bony and round. It looked a bit like one large bird beak.

DINO DETAILS:
Many herbivores used their bodies to protect themselves from enemies. They grew spikes, thick skin, or clubbed tails to keep away **predators**.

Minmi was covered in thick skin, like armor. It had curved bony spikes on its back for protection. It also had long legs which helped it run from its enemies.

Diamantinasaurus was a member of the titanosaur group of dinosaurs. It was one of the smaller members of this group. These dinosaurs lived near water, but stayed on land.

DINO DETAILS:
The biggest titanosaurs grew up to 115 feet (35 meters) long. The smallest only grew to be about 52 ft (16 m) long.

Dinosaurs lived millions of years ago, but their fossils tell us about how these creatures lived. Through learning what they ate, where they lived, and what their bodies looked like, we are able to better understand the history of Earth and the world around us.

Where Did the Dinosaurs Live?

Not many fossils have been found in Australia. But what has been found is exciting!

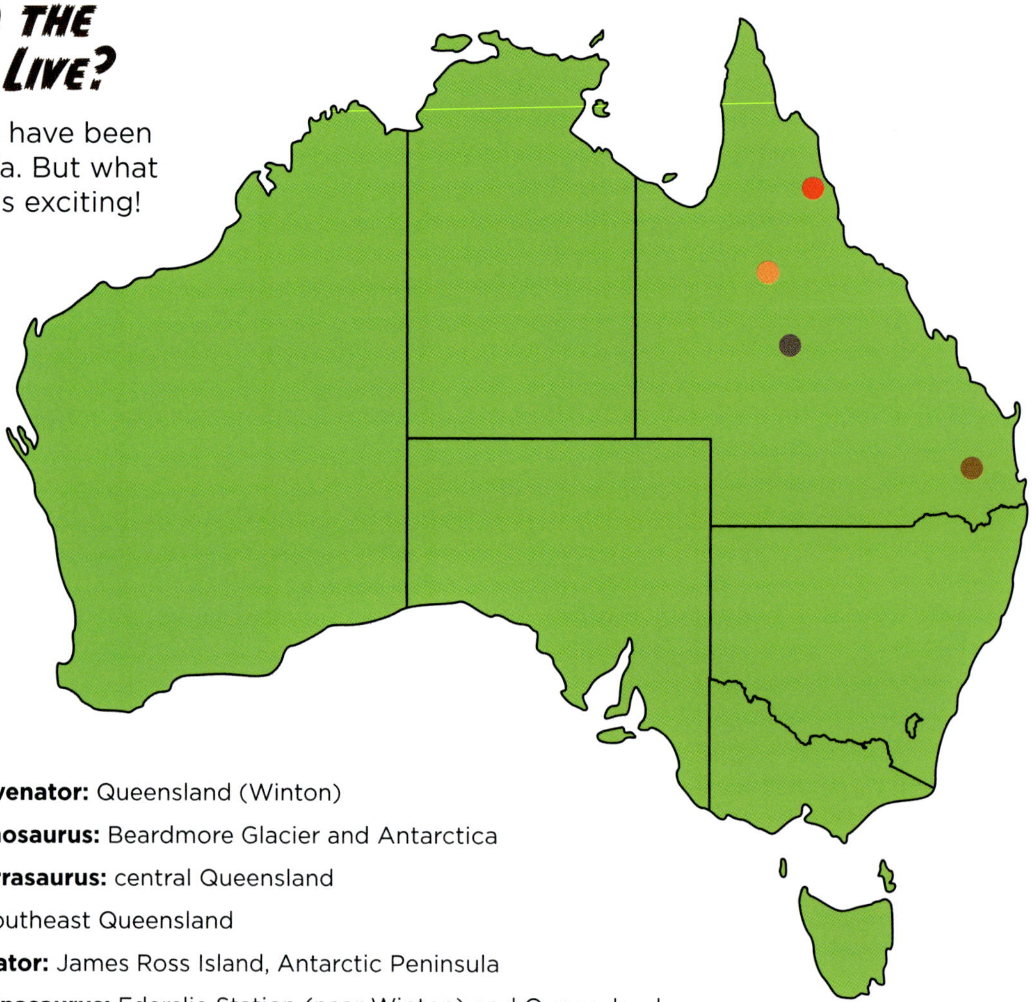

- **Australovenator:** Queensland (Winton)
- **Cryolophosaurus:** Beardmore Glacier and Antarctica
- **Muttaburrasaurus:** central Queensland
- **Minmi:** southeast Queensland
- **Imperobator:** James Ross Island, Antarctic Peninsula
- **Diamantinasaurus:** Ederslie Station (near Winton) and Queensland

Interesting Facts

- The word dinosaur means "terrible lizard."
- Many dinosaurs may have been covered in feathers.
- About 66 million years ago, a huge asteroid crashed into Earth that killed off all dinosaurs except for birds.
- Before dinosaurs, the Dimetrodon was the top predator of the ancient world.
- Most fossils are bones that have turned to stone.

Spotlight On: David Elliott

Imagine being in a field with a herd of sheep. You look down and see what appears to be an oddly shaped rock, only to find out it's really a fossil. Not just any fossil, the fossilized leg bone of the largest sauropod ever discovered on the Australian continent. That's exactly what happened to David Elliott back in 1999. Since then, he's found more fossilized dinosaur bones, including one of the most complete sauropod skeletons ever unearthed in Australia. Elliott and his wife Judy were instrumental in starting one of Australia's first dinosaur museums.

Glossary

carnivore (KAR-ni-vor):
A meat-eating animal

continent (KON-tin-ent):
One of the seven largest pieces of land on Earth

fossils (FAH-suhls):
Rock that forms after a living thing is preserved in the earth

herbivore (ER-buh-vor):
A plant-eating animal

predator (PRE-duh-ter):
An animal that hunts other animals for food

Index

Further Reading

Crane, Cody. *All About Fossils: Discovering Dinosaurs and Other Clues to the Past*. New York, NY: Scholastic, 2021.

Hansen, Grace. *Dinosaur Graveyards in Australia*. Minneapolis, MN: Abdo Kids, 2021.

Taylor, Charlotte. *Digging Up Dinosaur Fossils*.: Berkeley Heights, NJ: Enslow, 2021

On the Internet

Dinosaur Exhibition
https://australian.museum/exhibition/dinosaurs
Learn about the dinosaurs of Australia!.

Ology
https://www.amnh.org/explore/ology
Research dinosaurs on this kid-friendly website.